Interrupted Journey

Saving Endangered Sea Turtles

Kathryn Lasky

photographs by Christopher G. Knight

CANDLEWICK PRESS
CAMBRIDGE, MASSACHUSETTS

Text copyright ©2001
by Kathryn Lasky
Photographs copyright ©2001
by Christopher G. Knight

First edition 2001

Library of Congress
Cataloging-in-Publication Data

Lasky, Kathryn.
Interrupted journey ; saving endangered
sea turtles / Kathryn Lasky; illustrated by
Christopher G. Knight. — 1st ed.
p.   cm.
Summary: Describes efforts to protect sea
turtles, particularly Kemp's ridley turtles,
and help them reproduce and replenish
their once-dwindling numbers.

ISBN 0-7636-0635-9

1. Lepidochelys kempii—Juvenile literature.
2. Wildlife rescue—Juvenile literature.
[1. Atlantic ridley turtle. 2. Turtles. 3. Rare
animals. 4. Wildlife conservation.]
I. Knight, Christopher G., ill. II. Title.
QL666.C536 L37 2001
639.9'7792—dc21   99-057126

10 9 8 7 6 5 4 3 2 1

Printed in Hong Kong

This book was typeset
in Journal Text.

Candlewick Press
2067 Massachusetts Avenue
Cambridge, Massachusetts 02140

stranded

The young turtle has been swimming for three months now in the same warm shallow bay, grazing on small crabs and plankton, basking in an endless dream of calm water and plentiful food. But as the days begin to shorten and the light drains out of the sky earlier and earlier, the water grows colder. It drops to fifty degrees Fahrenheit. The turtle is confused. Swimming is harder. Its heartbeat slows—and almost stops.

Ten days before Thanksgiving, on a beach where Pilgrims once walked, Max Nolan, a ten-year-old boy, and his mother begin their patrol. The Nolans are among volunteers who walk Cape Cod's beaches during November and December to search for turtles who are often cold and stunned and seem dead—turtles whose lives they may be able to save.

It is a blustery day on Ellis Landing Beach. At twenty-five knots the bitter northwest wind stings Max's face like sharp needles. It makes his eyes water but he keeps looking— looking above the high-water mark through the clumps of seaweed, looking below the tide line where the sand is hard and sleek and lapped by surf—looking for a dark greenish-brown mound about the size of a pie plate, looking for a Kemp's ridley turtle that is dying and perhaps can be saved.

Max and his mother and the other volunteers work for a vital cause. All sea turtles are threatened or endangered; Kemp's ridleys are the most endangered of all. Right now on our planet there are fewer than eight thousand Kemp's ridley turtles left. They are a vanishing species.

On Ellis Landing Beach, snow squalls begin to whirl down. The waves are building, and as they begin to break, the white froth whips across their steep faces. So far there is no sign of a turtle.

Max is far ahead of his mother when he sees the hump in the sand being washed by the surf. He runs up to it and shouts to his mom, "Got one!" The turtle is cold. Its flippers are floppy. Its eyes are open, but the turtle is not moving at all. It might be dead, but then again, it might not.

Max remembers the instructions given to all rescuers. He picks up the turtle, which weighs about five pounds, and moves it above the high-tide mark to keep it from washing out to sea. Then he runs to find seaweed to protect it from the wind. He finds a stick to mark the spot, and next, he and his mother go to the nearest telephone and call the sea-turtle rescue line of the Massachusetts Audubon Society.

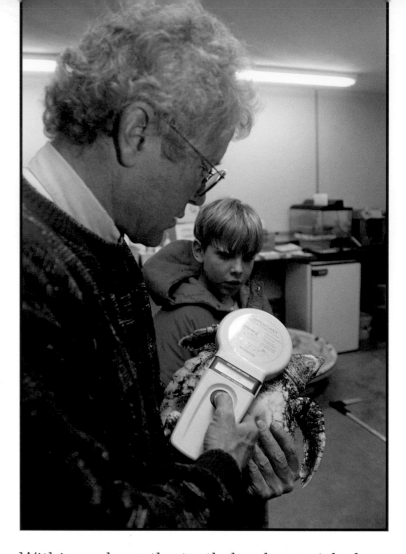

Within an hour the turtle has been picked up and taken to the Wellfleet Bay Wildlife Sanctuary on Cape Cod. Robert Prescott, the director of the Sanctuary, examines the turtle. "It sure does look dead," he says softly. "But you never can tell." If the turtle is really alive, it must be brought out of its cold, stunned condition. That is a task for the New England Aquarium with its medical team who, over the years, have made a specialty of treating turtles.

Robert puts the new turtle in a plastic wading pool with another turtle that is quite lively. Max crouches by the edge and watches his turtle. It is as still as a stone. He gently touches a flipper. Nothing moves. Then after about twenty minutes, he thinks he might see a flicker in the turtle's left eyelid. He leans closer. "Hey, it's moving!" It wasn't just the eyelid. He saw the right rear flipper move a fraction of an inch. Over the next five minutes, he sees the turtle make three or four microscopically small motions with its right rear flipper. Soon, the rescue team from the New England Aquarium arrives.

emergency

Beth Chittick is a vet at the New England Aquarium. When the turtles arrive she is ready for them. The turtles are taken immediately into the examination room. Beth is joined by head veterinarian, Howard Crum. They insert a thermometer into the cloaca, the opening under the turtle's tail. The temperature of the turtle Max found is fifty degrees Fahrenheit. Normal temperature for a turtle is usually about seventy-five degrees. Howard next tries to find a heartbeat. He listens intently. "I think I can hear a faint sound . . ." He holds the stiff turtle against his ear as one might hold a seashell. "Why, gee whiz, I can hear the ocean," he jokes.

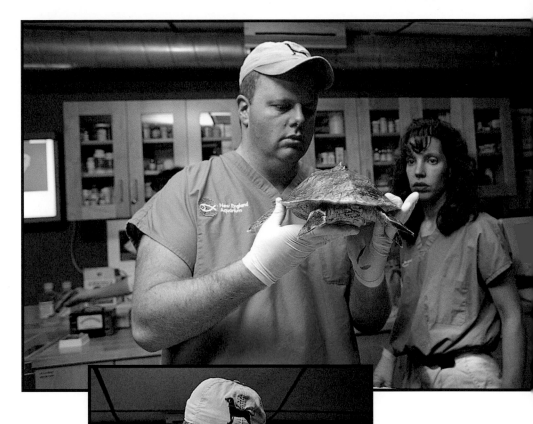

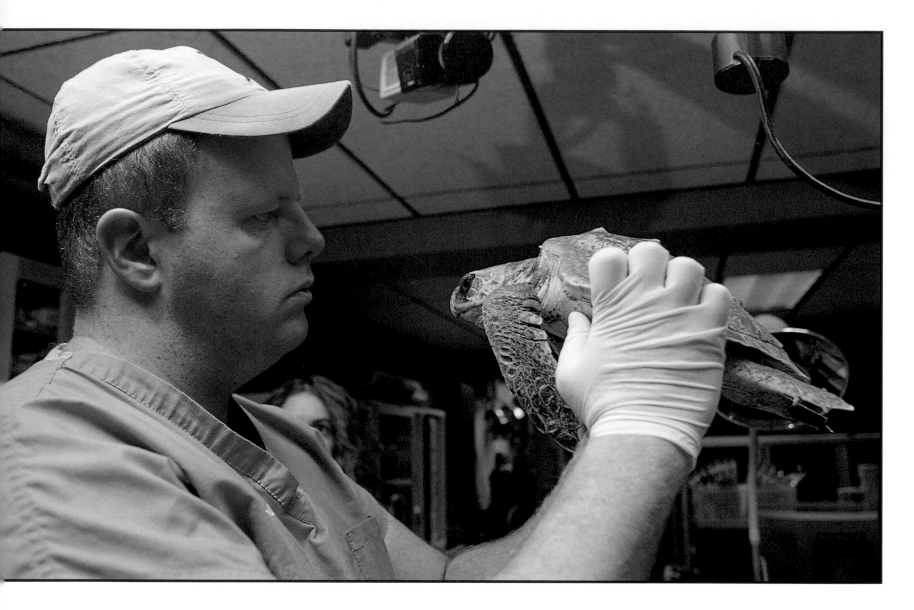

Howard is still not convinced that the turtle is dead. "With turtles," Howard says, "death is a relative term." Turtles can operate, can survive, even when their hearts slow down for periods of time. Events that might damage the larger, more complicated brains of other animals will not always prove fatal to turtles.

In fact, a turtle's heartbeat naturally slows down at times to just one or two beats per minute in order to conserve oxygen and keep vital organs like the brain working. So Howard won't give up on this turtle yet. The turtle does not seem dehydrated. The skin on its limbs is not wrinkled—a good sign.

An assistant swabs down an area on the turtle's neck, from which a blood sample will be taken. By analyzing the blood, Howard and Beth will be able to see how the turtle's kidneys and other organs are functioning.

Next the turtle is cleaned. The algae are washed and wiped from its shell. The doctors detect movement in its tail and then see some of the same movements that Max saw in its flippers. They are the motions a turtle makes when it swims. They do not necessarily mean that it is alive, though. It has been speculated that these movements could be what are sometimes called vestigial motions, echoes of long-ago actions, fossil behaviors embedded in the brain of an ancient creature. The turtle could be swimming in death or swimming toward life.

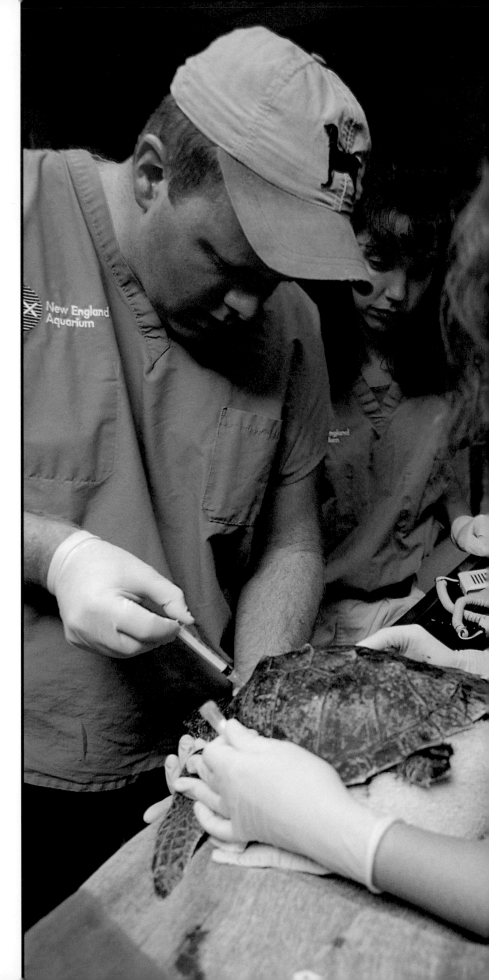

Nonetheless, the vets hook up the turtle to an intravenous needle through which fluids will be pumped very slowly at a temperature slightly higher than the turtle's body. Beth and Howard have learned much about the condition of this turtle but they are still not sure if it is really alive or dead.

Finally the turtle is tagged with a yellow-blue band. It will be known as Yellow-Blue. It is put in the Intensive Care Unit, a large temperature-controlled stainless steel box with a glass window. Inside, the turtle is placed on a soft pile of towels so its shell is supported and it will not have to rest on its ventrum, or bottom shell.

Then the team turn their attention to another turtle, which is definitely alive. Howard picks up the turtle and talks to it as its flippers thrash madly. "Okay, little man!" This turtle's temperature is sixty-two degrees. When they take its blood, the sample appears much redder than the nearly brownish blood of Yellow-Blue, which indicates that there is more oxygen in it.

But as lively as this one is, Howard gives it only a fifty-percent survival rate. There is a good chance that pneumonia could still develop. They insert an intravenous tube for rehydration. Then they tag the animal with a plain yellow band.

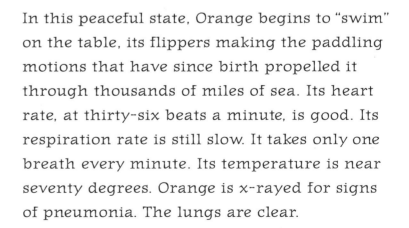

There are other turtles also being treated. One, Orange, needs to have its eyes lubricated and then be weighed and examined. The turtle is feisty and needs to be sedated. This is done without drugs, simply by shielding the top of its head from the ceiling lights. There is a gland inside a turtle's head that is sensitive to light, and it is speculated that when the gland is covered, it helps the turtle settle down into a relaxed, near-sleeping state.

In this peaceful state, Orange begins to "swim" on the table, its flippers making the paddling motions that have since birth propelled it through thousands of miles of sea. Its heart rate, at thirty-six beats a minute, is good. Its respiration rate is still slow. It takes only one breath every minute. Its temperature is near seventy degrees. Orange is x-rayed for signs of pneumonia. The lungs are clear.

Whatever the outcome for these three turtles, Beth, Howard, Robert, Max, and his mother all know they are doing their part to help return the turtles to health, to help return them to the sea.

risky life

Release of the turtles into the ocean again is the goal for the New England Aquarium. But still, there are many hazards awaiting a healthy released turtle.

Humans represent the worst hazard for sea turtles and are, shockingly, one of the main causes of death of juvenile and mature turtles. Many of these deaths are accidental—turtles can get caught in the lines and nets of fishing boats, and sometimes they are hit by the careless drivers of speedboats or other tourist craft. Another cause is deliberate slaughter by people, for turtle meat is valued, and their shells, from which tortoiseshell articles are made, often command a high price.

But the dangers begin even before the baby turtles hatch. Turtle eggs, laid on the sandy beaches of Rancho Nuevo in Mexico, are considered a delicacy and are even thought to have health benefits. So sometimes poachers go out and raid the nests for eggs. If a nest survives and the eggs actually do hatch, a baby sea turtle's first job is to get out of the deep sandy shaft its mother has dug and refilled, and get to the sea for its long ocean journey.

If it hatches during the day, predators, birds in particular, are the main problem. At night, if the beach is in a developed area, buildings and streetlights are a major cause of hatchling death. The baby turtles become confused and disoriented by the lights. Instead of heading toward the surf, they head toward civilization— streets, highways, cars. They get smashed.

If there are no human hazards, there are night predators. Between the nest and the tide line, ghost crabs wait to snatch the baby turtles with their claws. And if the hatchlings do make it to the water and past the breaking surf, there are always sharks and other predatory fish.

But if they are lucky hatchlings and encounter a tangle of seaweed, they might indeed survive and spend at least a year drifting about on the weed mats that float atop the billowy waves of the high seas. The seaweed snares food for the baby turtles—crustaceans, jellyfish, and small shrimp. Suppose a baby turtle does make it to, say, the age of two or three (a juvenile). What happens then?

Yellow-Blue and most of the other turtles that washed up on the beaches of Cape Cod were juvenile Kemp's ridley turtles. They were two to three years old. Like all turtles, in their entire lifetime they have never interacted with their parents or sisters or brothers. They are solitary from birth. There is no one to teach them anything. They live alone, and they live by instinct.

It is instinct that took their mothers to the beaches of Rancho Nuevo on the Gulf of Mexico to lay their eggs. And it is instinct that draws the juveniles to swim east out into the Gulf of Mexico. Some end up in the Sargasso Sea, which is rich in food. They love the small snails, the leafy parts of the grassy seaweed called sargassum, the plankton, the small crabs, and even the plankton eggs.

Some juveniles, however, swim into what is called the Loop Current, which sweeps south around the tip of Florida and then north into the Gulf Stream—a current of warm water that flows up the east coast of the United States. Often the turtles are lured into the maze of the shallow warm bays of Cape Cod. Possibly attracted by the abundance of food, the turtles find them-selves in the wrong place, their journey interrupted.

Even though Cape Cod is not the Sargasso Sea, it is still a turtle dream. These protected and shallow waters stay warmer longer than those outside the long bent arm of the Cape. Some turtles stay there until November, and then it is too late.

It is usually juvenile Kemp's ridleys that are stranded on the Cape beaches. Older, larger turtles have different migration habits and do not, therefore, find themselves in these waters.

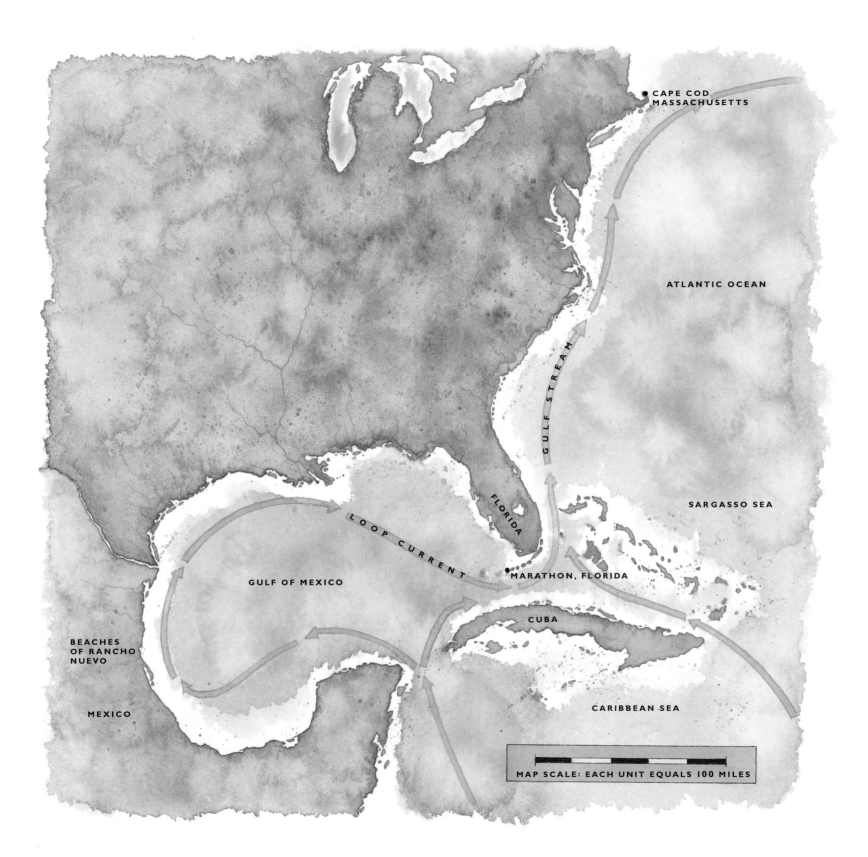

CAPE COD
MASSACHUSETTS

ATLANTIC OCEAN

GULF STREAM

FLORIDA

SARGASSO SEA

LOOP CURRENT

GULF OF MEXICO

MARATHON, FLORIDA

CUBA

BEACHES
OF RANCHO
NUEVO

MEXICO

CARIBBEAN SEA

MAP SCALE: EACH UNIT EQUALS 100 MILES

Back at the New England Aquarium, things are looking up for Yellow-Blue and half a dozen others. Every day these turtles are growing stronger in the medical center. Yellow-Blue is recovering well. Over the next few weeks it is reintroduced to water in a small tank. However, when the turtle is first put back in the water, a technician must hold it half in and half out of the water. Once the turtle begins moving its flippers steadily, it is ready to support itself. Someone still watches, though, to make sure that it can keep its head above water. When the turtle can eat solid food, a technician hand-feeds it, holding tongs with a turtle's favorite snacks—small live crab, or pieces of herring and squid.

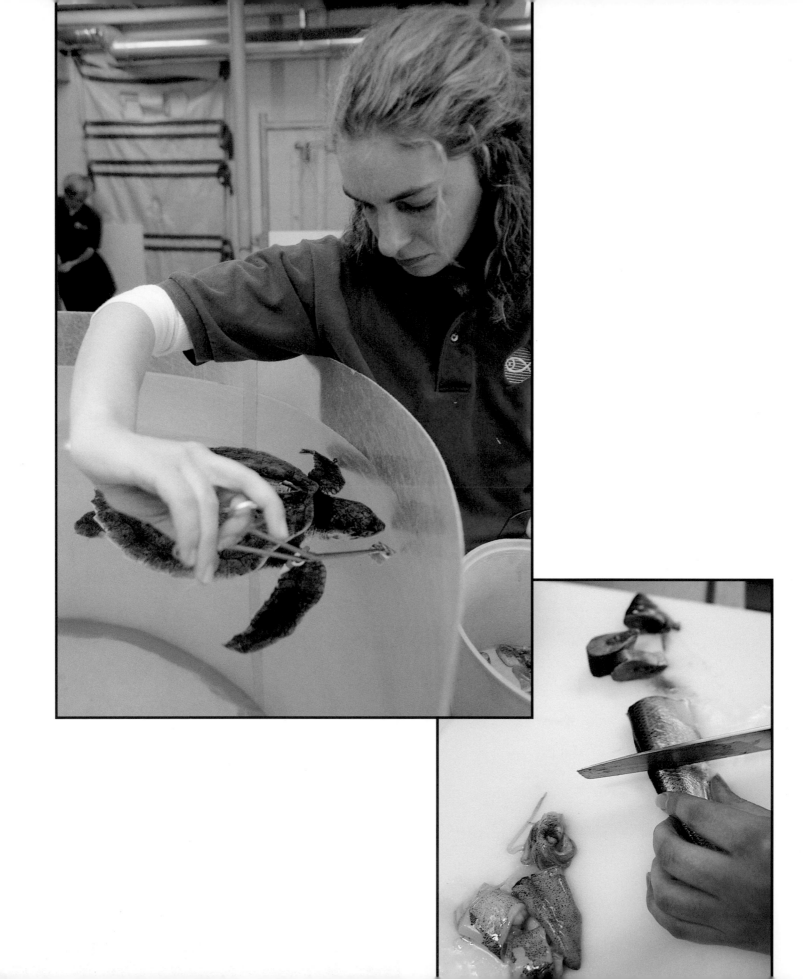

release

On a windy spring morning in April, five months after it was found, **Yellow-Blue is taken from its small tank in the New England Aquarium and put into a plastic box with wet towels.** Yellow-Blue has recovered from its ordeal. But for the first leg of its journey it will not swim—Yellow-Blue will fly. A small cargo jet will take the turtle to The Turtle Hospital in Marathon, in the Florida Keys.

Richie Moretti is the owner, director, and founder of the hospital. He is not a veterinarian. He is not a marine biologist. He is a man who loves turtles, and his calling in life is to help injured animals. In order to do this, Richie runs Hidden Harbor, a motel. With the money he makes from the motel, he runs the hospital.

The people who come to the motel can no longer swim in the motel pool. It is filled with injured sea turtles—loggerheads, green turtles, Kemp's ridleys, and hawksbills. Guests cannot even sunbathe or sit around the pool, for there are smaller tanks for baby and juvenile turtles not big enough, or too sick, to swim in the big pool. Veterinarians and volunteers come to the hospital to work with the turtles.

On the day of the release, Richie and his assistant remove Yellow-Blue from the tank and attach a permanent metal tag to its flipper so that the turtle can be tracked throughout its sea voyage. The turtle is feisty and flaps its flippers, perhaps sensing that something exciting is about to happen. Richie and his crew load Yellow-Blue and several larger turtles into his high-speed, shallow-bottomed boat. Before departing from the pier, Richie checks the charts of the waters around the southern keys. He wants to take Yellow-Blue to the quietest, calmest, and safest waters he knows—a place where there are no tourists racing around in speedboats or fishing boats or shrimp trawlers. He wants this turtle to have a fair chance of swimming out to the Sargasso Sea without getting hit by a boat, chopped by a propeller, or tangled in the deadly nets and lines of fishermen. They put Yellow-Blue in a box, cover its shell with wet towels, and then roar out into Florida Bay.

The boat goes fast, close to sixty miles an hour. Soon they are forty miles to the south and west. They are on the very most outlying keys of the Gulf side. The waters are shallow and calm. They cut the boat's engine and now the water is so shallow that Richie raises the outboard motor and poles in to what he considers the perfect place to release Yellow-Blue. It is in the still waters of a cove off a key named Content. Susan, a volunteer, lifts Yellow-Blue from its box and holds it half-in, half-out of the water. "Oh, you want to go! You want to go! Hang on, fella! Let's get used to things!"

Then she lowers Yellow-Blue so it is completely underwater. The flippers beat, and finally Susan's hands let go! Yellow-Blue streaks through the turquoise water, leaving a curling wake of bubbles. "So long, buddy," Richie calls. "Stay away from fishing lines. Don't get hit by any propellers." Richie and his volunteers feel an odd mixture of emotions. It is thrilling to see a turtle once injured and captive swim free through the crystal clear waters. But it is also scary: what is the future for this turtle?

What's waiting out there for Yellow-Blue, and the loggerhead and hawksbill turtles they are also releasing? Richie tries to think of the good things. A rich sea, thick with mats of seaweed delivering up plankton, hermit and spider crabs, whelks and moon shells, mussels and squid, like the ocean's most lavish turtle buffet. A mate, or mates, somewhere, with whom Yellow-Blue will couple, insuring a clutch of Kemp's ridley eggs in a nest on a beach.

It is a desperate cause, but Richie is a believing man. He turns the boat back, poles to the open water, and then heads for home. Guests are due at the motel. If the occupancy rate is high through the off-season, Richie will be able to afford some new x-ray equipment for the hospital.

miracles

There is an immense beach on the Gulf of Mexico below the Texas border that is perfect for nesting turtles. Fifty years ago, at a certain time of year, there was not a patch of sand visible. The beach would appear paved with turtles, and the surf would be churning with turtles—Kemp's ridleys thrashing, tumbling, swimming ashore. More than 40,000 females had been mysteriously, inexorably drawn back to the beach where they had hatched perhaps eight years before. They were now sexually mature. They had mated often with several males and returned to this beach to lay their eggs. In one nest, a female might deposit 100 eggs. The sex of the turtle is determined by the temperature of the location of its egg in the nest. Not every egg would hatch and not every hatchling would make it to maturity, but with 40,000 females laying nearly four million eggs, the Kemp's ridley's future seemed secure—even with poachers, shrimp boats, and ocean pollution.

But by 1974, only 2,500 Kemp's ridley turtles came ashore on the same beach in Mexico. A few years later there were fewer than one thousand. And suddenly there were scarcely

five hundred Kemp's ridleys left in the entire world. It was in 1978 that Mexico and the United States began in earnest a program to save Kemp's ridleys.

Milagroso. Un milagro grande. Miraculous. A great miracle. These words are often heard now on the beaches of Rancho Nuevo in the Tamaulipas state of Mexico. Since the program began, the number of returning females has increased. In the last ten years the numbers have risen steadily. Now over three thousand turtles return each year. Five times the population in 1978. It is a miracle.

The beach is hardly paved with turtles, but in late May almost *every* day females arrive. If many arrive, if it is a true *arribada* with scores of turtles crawling out of the surf and up onto the beach in a single day, the volunteers must race to them in their beach buggies. Once they sight a nesting female, there are tags to be attached or perhaps tags already there to be read.

Measurements must be taken and the eggs collected to bring back to the safety of the corrals where new nests will be dug.

The female turtle is patient through all of this. Very little distracts her from digging her nest. The work is hard, for the turtle is a sea creature, not one of the land. She uses her swimming motions, flicking out the sand with her hind flippers until there is a shaft perhaps thirty inches deep into which she deposits her eggs. Her eyes are caked with sand, and often she secretes thick tears to clear them, which makes her look as if she is weeping. Her shell seems to be the color of every ocean she has ever swum in, from the dark green-brown of the New England coast to the faded turquoise of the Caribbean.

When she has finished, she sweeps the
sand back into the shaft to cover the eggs,
then rocks violently from side to side
to tamp down the sand with
the edges of her shell. She
has not learned this.
She has never seen
her mother do it.
She has never seen
her mother at all.
It is instinct, and
then she turns to the
sea. She really is not
meant for land, and it
seems like some odd trick
of nature that it is only on land
that she can lay her eggs. It takes her several
minutes to heave herself down to the surf.

There is a track left in the sand from her flippers and tail. By the next tide it will have
vanished. The turtle herself will return several
more times during the nesting season to lay
more clutches of eggs.

The volunteers will try to find and transport as many clutches as possible to their corrals. Already they have nearly one thousand in one of the corrals on the main beach of Rancho Nuevo. As they near the moment of hatching, after six to twelve weeks of incubation, these corrals are covered with fine mesh cloth to keep out birds and other predators.

As the time for hatching draws near, the volunteers check the nests several times a day. It is an exciting moment and they want to be sure to get the turtles to the water as quickly as possible, so that each hatchling has a fighting chance. As they emerge from the nests in the corral, the volunteers scoop them up and take them in boxes down to the water's edge.

When they hatch, they must dig up and out of their sandy shafts. The sand above the hatchlings is picked away and falls on the hatchlings below. It is a climb of almost three feet for some. They crawl up and over one another. All their squirming and wriggling together in order to crawl out helps loosen the sand. It is the only thing these turtles will ever do socially as a group. From the moment they are out of their nests, they will live the most solitary lives of almost any animal on earth, coming together again only to mate.

It is a few minutes after dawn. The sky is pale, but when the sun rises, clouds stream just above the horizon like tatters of torn pink silk. The sea is calm. There is barely any surf. Where a curling line of lacy foam swags the hard wet sand, dozens of small dark shapes about the size of half-dollars are picked up, spun about, and then set down again. Because Gustave, a volunteer, is watching over them, no bird would dare approach. The hatchlings are exhausted because they have spent the hours before dawn thrashing their way up and out of the nest. The water, though gentle and calm, sometimes flips them onto their backs. Even then, they do not panic or thrash the air with their tiny flippers. They are simply too tired. Gustave quickly turns them right side up again.

Gradually, through the first hour of the morning, the hatchlings begin to stir. Slowly, as the salt water combs over them, some dim signal, some ancient urge, a mysterious impulse, begins to glow faintly in their very small brains. First one turtle then another seems to wake. Their little flippers, no bigger than the tips of popsicle sticks, begin their swimming motions. They don't need to practice. They know how to do it.

By the time they are a few yards from shore, they are fully alert and in a swimming frenzy. They will swim almost continuously through their first day and night if they do not encounter a shark. If they are really lucky, they might fetch up on a mat of seaweed and drift about for days and even months with a ready supply of food.

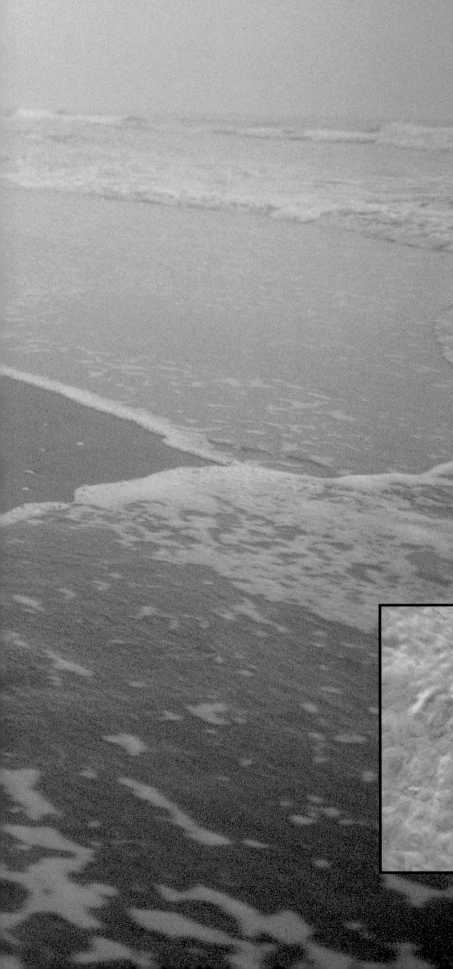

The forty-five hatchlings, weighing no more than seventeen grams each, measuring no longer than two-and-a-half inches and with heads smaller than peanuts, will disappear into the sea and rarely, if ever, be seen again until they are juveniles, about five pounds and perhaps ten inches in length and two to three years old. No one is quite sure where they go. But for the first few minutes after they are released into the calm waters, now gilded pink by the rising sun, the hatchlings swim madly, their dark little heads bobbing out of the water, the churning flippers so small hardly a bubble is left in their wakes. They are swimming toward deeper water, toward unknown seas, fierce in their instinct, alone in their quest for life.